The Lost Art of
DOS
Commands

Authored By

Daniel Valencia
&
Jordan Kaufman

Copyright © 2016 The Six Figure Teen Trust
All rights reserved.
ISBN-10: 1539933938
ISBN-13: 978-1539933939

DEDICATION (FROM DANIEL)

To my father, Dean Valencia,
Who worked so hard to give us a better life.
Thank you.

DANIEL VALENCIA

CONTENTS

The Lost Art of DOS Commands 5
    The Birth and History of DOS. 5
    DOS – How It Was Lost 9
    GUI – The New Dominant 15
    DOS – The Light That Was Never Shut Out 19
    DOS – A True Art 23
CONCLUSION 52
ABOUT THE AUTHOR 56

The Lost Art of DOS Commands

The Birth and History of DOS.

Short for **Microsoft Disk Operating System, MS-DOS**, is a non-graphical command line system derived from the 86-DOS which was originally created for IBM compatible computers. MS-DOS was originally written by Tim Paterson, and was introduced to the world by Microsoft; When IBM first launched its revolutionary personal computer, the IBM PC, in August of 1981. It came with a 16-bit operating system from Microsoft, MS-DOS 1.0. This was Microsoft's first operating system, and it also became the first widely used operating system for the IBM PC and its clones. Believe it or not MS-DOS 1.0 was merely a renamed version of what was known as QDOS (Quick and Dirty Operating System), which Microsoft ended up buying from a company in Seattle.

QDOS was developed as a clone of the CP/M (Control Program for Microcomputers) eight-bit operating system to provide compatibility with popular business applications at the time, which were known as WordStar, and dBase. CP/M was written by Gary Kildall. Bill Gates, the co-founder of Microsoft, persuaded IBM to let his company have marketing rights for the operating system separately from the IBM PC project. Microsoft renamed it PC-DOS (the IBM version) and MS-DOS (the Microsoft version).

The two versions were initially nearly identical, but they eventually diverged. At that time the use of disks for storing the operating system and data was considered cutting edge technology. Until its acquisition of QDOS, Microsoft had been mainly a vendor of computer programming languages. Gates and co-founder Paul Allen had written Microsoft Basic and were selling it on disks and tapes mostly to PC hobbyists. MS-DOS soared in popularity with the surge in the PC market.

Revenue from its sales fueled Microsoft's phenomenal growth, and MS-DOS was the key to company's rapid emergence as the dominant firm in the software industry. This product continued to be the largest single contributor to Microsoft's income well after it had become more famous for Windows. Subsequent versions of MS-DOS featured improved performance and additional functions, not a few of which were copied from other operating systems. For example, version 1.25, which was released in 1982, added support for double-sided disks, which eliminated the need to manually turn the disks over to access the reverse side. Version 2.0, released the next year, added support for directories for IBM's then huge 10MB hard disk drive (HDD) and for 360KB, 5.25-inch floppy disks.

This was followed by version 2.11 later in the same year, which added support for foreign and extended characters. Version 3.0 launched in 1984, added support for 1.2MB floppy disks and 32MB HDDs. This was soon followed by version 3.1, which added support for networks. Additions and improvements in subsequent versions included support for multiple HDD partitions, for disk compression and for larger partitions as well as an improved disk-checking utility, enhanced memory management, a disk defragmenter and an improved text editor. The final major version was 7.0, which was released in 1995 as part of Microsoft Windows 95.

Windows 95 featured close integration with that operating system, including support for long filenames and the removal of numerous utilities, some of which were on the Windows 95 CDROM. It was revised in 1997 with version 7.1, which added support for the FAT32 file system on HDDs. Although many of the features were copied from UNIX, MS-DOS was never able to come anywhere close to UNIX in terms of performance or features. For example, MS-DOS never became a serious multi-user or multitasking operating system (both of which were core features of UNIX right from the start) in spite of attempts to retrofit these capabilities. To this day, it is well debated, and discussed rather Windows, Linux (UNIX), or MAC-OSX (also UNIX) is the right operating system.

In all reality however, these operating systems accomplish most of the goals, and tasks needed in a daily life-style, some better than others. Rationally, these operating systems, and what they have to offer, are of a preference as to what you want your computer to be like, what you want it to do, and how well you want it to perform. For instance, if you want to do some gaming on a reliable machine, then a tank, or technically called a "Thick Client" would be the way to go, and most of the time, these Thick Clients work best with

Windows. Where-as a more light-weight, or technically called a "Thin Client" would fit better with Linux, but obviously wouldn't be used for the intent of gaming, or anything graphically intensive. I myself, have a beast machine running Windows 7 Ultimate. (Her name is Sasha.)

Anyways...

DOS – How It Was Lost

Things have changed over time, though. Today, there have been numerous allegations of the death of the command line interface after windows 7. It has been claimed to be "outdated". The disk operating system, DOS, is the computer operating system that uses the command line. DOS was most commonly used during the 1980s and 1990s. In fact, DOS was praised for a long time, for at the time, it was considered cutting-edge technology. However, this sadly, isn't the case anymore. It's been becoming more, and more noticeable the absence of people who are actually acquainted the command line, the vast majority, today, don't even know the terms "Terminal", "DOS", or "Command-Line-Interface", and to be honest, it's disappointing.

With the world ever changing, and the constantly evolving technology, it's all too easy to forget the roots of what got us to today. (I mean I'm sure that MS-DOS isn't the ultimate grand-pappy of operating systems, but I'd say it's important to be acquainted with).With the release of oncoming Windows operating systems, such as Windows 8, 8.1, and recently, 10, today's generation, and even people who have used DOS, and appreciated it, are starting to fade, and here's why.

Decline in the use of DOS started in the mid-1990s when Microsoft released Windows 95 which did not require a separate DOS license. Since then, the advancement in computer technology has forced companies like Microsoft to push the command line aside as easier and faster troubleshooting methods are developed. Developers such as Microsoft, Apple, and others are eliminating the command line from the equation, making it appear out of sight, and making it easier to forget, in order to make use of their operating systems easier to use, mainly to appease their consumers. As a result the main consumer base for these flagship operating systems, are those of which that have not acquainted themselves with the famous DOS. This has caused the perception of DOS to be irrelevant, or even with some, people, non-existent, or is used by people who want to hack, and thus have malicious intent. As a result it makes it seem like rocket science to general users to troubleshoot their system, or that they need to take their PC in to a professional to fix a simple issue.

Now, I can hear a lot of people thinking, and debating in their heads, with this subject, because in some cases it is totally legitimate, and necessary to take your computer in to a professional. This is not something I am trying to advertise as a bad thing. I am appealing to the cases in which people don't *want* to learn how to use to command line. Though even this case has it's reasons such as a lack of time, it comes off as intimidating to learn something like the command line, and that is something I personally, am not okay with. I believe that knowing the command line is a basic essential to using, or owning a computer. It isn't too hard to learn, nor should it be intimidating, thus, anyone who wants to learn it, should learn it.

In reality though, this mentality is used as a marketing tactic. For it is true, that people who are good at what they do, such as IT professionals, or Electrical Technicians earn their incomes based off of the ignorance, or lack of interest or time, of their own customers. Think about it, if you knew how to fix "NTLDR is missing" you surely wouldn't take your computer to anyone for them to fix it. You'd already know that that error is caused by an inability to load, or locate the boot-loader for Windows. You'd also know that the command line would greatly help you resolve this issue.

Thus, in a typical situation, a computer technician, or a profession wouldn't gain any profit, at least in the retail area. Admittedly, I haven't heard or seen of a situation where someone, other than me, of course, was able to fix their own computer issues. In a world where the art of DOS is slowing fading into a slow death, this is to be expected. This isn't really an issue that's going to go anywhere substantial, though. If I had to predict what was going to happen in the next couple years, I'd say either DOS rose to its deserved fame, or died in an obscurity.

Hey, the world is run on computers, and therefore executed commands, so if you're looking for a profession, why not hop aboard the multi-billion dollar industry, and start making the big bucks? It's safe to say that it is inevitable that if you want to protect yourself more than you already have in the world of computers, you need to acquire knowledge of the famous command line. In many ways knowing the art of DOS will complement you, protect you, and reward you. I'll explain why in more detail later in this book. In short, though, the steady upholding of these illusions and mentalities has, in a way, killed MS-DOS's prevalence.

The Graphical user interface (GUI) is most recent interface that is perceived to replace DOS. The interface uses windows, menus, visual indicators and graphical icons. This offers easier navigation than the text-based command line interface which was considered at the time challenging to master. The GUI allows interaction with the electronic devices through direct manipulation. Human interaction uses the keyboard and mouse to perform the basic functions. The keyboard offers shortcuts to functions, sticky keys and other functions. In this case, the interaction settings are pre-set by the creator of the computing devices.

The use of GUI aims at making it as easy as possible for users of the computer or other electronic devices to understand and operate their devices. The simplicity of the GUI makes the use of the command line interface less important to those who are not interested in learning how to utilize maximum performance from their devices. There are numerous functions that the GUI interface does not offer as they may be deemed too technical for the users. These functions are mostly left out for experts and technicians.

Now when it comes to GUI, I have to say myself, that I thoroughly enjoy the creative and innovative user interfaces. The rise of GUI started back when Windows 95 was released, which did not require a separate DOS license. From there on the future of windows was broad in the light of GUI, and when other distributions started rolling out, Microsoft started to find more, and more innovative, clever, ways to make use of windows a lot easier than it ever was before. Let it be known that this was the start of a very new and different era for computers, technology, and thus, Windows, as Microsoft was moving forward with their flagship operating system, Windows.

It can be well said, that the rise of the graphical user interface had a hand in the alleged death of the command line. This makes a lot of sense, as when the user interface first was introduced, it was pretty, and it was fluent, and easier, thus more productive. The GUI actually had a huge influence on Microsoft's future products, as it's new, and innovative GUI took the entire industry by storm.

Even today you see Microsoft's ideas for their GUI, as they sinned against the industry with the releases of the infamous windows 8 by removing the start button, but later added it back, in Windows 8.1, thus granting them forgiveness. If I had preference myself, I would have a healthy mix of GUI, and command line use, I've even had first-hand experience creating my own custom GUI within PC video games with the programming language LUA.

The reason why most people shy away from learning the CLI is due to the steep learning curve that is involved in learning the interface use. One needs to master many commands for each action. Users do not need knowledge of any programming languages in order to use GUI. However, as we are about to learn, both interfaces are important and quite simple to use as long as the user understands which is best suited for a particular task. Moreover, both interfaces are available for Windows PC users. DOS is also used to enable use of duplicate programs such Linux.

GUI – The New Dominant

While we cannot dispute the importance of the GUI interface in computing, neither water down the impact that the interface has had in computing, it cannot be considered as a replacement to the command prompt; rather, it is a supplement that should enhance the user experience. The art of DOS command is losing its importance and role in the modern world for a variety of reasons, most of which can be attributed to advancement in technology. The ease of use of the GUI interface makes people lose the interest in learning how to use the command line interface. However, the GUI interface does not offer as many capabilities as the command prompt.

The art in GUI is generally described in terms of the appearance. With the spontaneous growth in the number of programmers and ease of creating programs, the aesthetic appearance of the programs has become an important aspect when choosing which one to use. The use of visual art simply incorporates art to the software and gives a good appearance which pleases the user. In this case, the art is simply incorporated to harmonize the features that are to be displayed. The functions that are represented by the graphics are of the most importance to the user even though most do not bother what happens to make the icons and other graphics to function as they do. As long as the users are not bored, they are fine. This is what leads the websites and programs to changing designs often to keep the users interested.

To me, it would behove everyone to know that the very fundamentals of Windows, Linux, or even OSX are what make up today's known famous operating systems. I personally have come to the conclusion that it helps one to not only gain more knowledge, but to become more appreciative of the hard work, forethought, and execution that it takes to put together one of these beautiful things we know as, an operating system.

Think of it as the mediator to what you need or want and the resources that a computer has to offer. For instance: You simply cannot take advantage of a powerful GPU without the likes of an operating system. To put simply, the computer is much like a body, requiring many parts that do many different things to come together to accomplish many things.

The beautiful part is though, is that none of that could ever be accomplished without someone, or something telling the computer to do just that, in other words, an operating system. You need an operating system of manage your components, and serve as the basic input, output system for basic tasks such as renaming, moving, creating, or deleting a file, or folder.

There are many arguments that revolve around which is the best interface for the user. Similarly, both DOS and GUI interfaces have good reputations and advantages to the users. Therefore, it is prudent to say that what needs to happen is have a middle ground. In the modern computing systems, the two technologies are available for the user to exploit. The user should exploit the advantages in each of the products in order to get the best experience from their devices.

The biggest hindrance to the use of the command line prompt is the steep learning curve involved in mastering the commands. The commands are easy to use and one can start by learning them through practice. In the windows PC created in the modern day, the cmd should not be as hidden as it is now so that more users are aware of its existence, hence provoke their curiosity to learn what it does. Since the commands are constant, the offline help information should also include the command prompts so that a user is able to access the commands they need to use for any functions.

Windows operating systems have diagnosis processes that try (mostly in vain) to troubleshoot system and network errors. If the command prompt is given to the users as part of the diagnosis and including the commands necessary for the specific problem, the users can be able to solve many issues that they have with their computers.

When the steps are taken to reclaim the necessity of DOS commands in computing, the art of DOS will be reclaimed. It will enhance creativity as programmers and users will begin using it to create new functionalities, especially with the modern computers which have more processing power. A person will be able to protect their computer from attacks which could be important for them. Additionally, the skills of using the command prompt are very important in a working environment.

The systems often require the use of the command prompt

for a variety of activities. Since these are simple troubleshooting tasks, they may be skills that are fundamental for all employees. This is similar to the need for people to learn at least basic computer skills in order to secure a job at any position. The basic skills are usually knowledge of operation using the GUI interface. It is important for people to learn the lost art before it reappears and they find themselves in a disadvantage as they lack the necessary skills.

DOS – The Light That Was Never Shut Out

DOS - What has happened to it? Well, a lot of things happened to it. There were a lot of contributing factors as to why the light of DOS was dimmed to the point of near darkness. DOS, though, never did fully die out. It's still used, by a certain group of people. People like me. These people are easily considered either nerds, experts, or professionals, as these kinds of people are prone to have more experience, and expertise in DOS, and general troubleshooting, in the windows, or even Linux environment than the average user.

Sadly, to the average user, DOS doesn't really exist, because it's been hidden from them. Though, I'm not trying to say that developers trying to suppress the command line, they're just tucking it away in a safe place, so it doesn't get noticed. With good reason, too, after all, they have a huge consumer base to appease, and uphold, and sadly the vast majority of this consumer base is made up of people who couldn't really care less about the command line. The good news though, is that DOS still lives through modern windows as the command prompt (or command line).

For those who have the notion that DOS was phased out of Windows, search for "cmd" in the windows search tool and you will find the command line. This is DOS, but a really limited version of it, compared to what it used to be. You can still do most of the things you were able to do before, it just grew different over time. The command line serves today, as the legacy of DOS, and is being carried on, with good spirit, by the community surrounding it.

DOS still has a pretty decent user base. There are still people out there, and tutorials being made by those people, on how to do this, or that, on the command line. Linux, has a huge base when it comes to servers, mainly operated from a command line, rather it be local, or remote, via SSH. MACOSX hasn't really done anything notable, other than just exist, so I don't have anything to say about it, other than the fact, that I don't like apple products, and therefore Macintosh. Either way DOS still lives through its legacy, the command line.

A restoration of the command line started a couple years back from now, when video game servers, started to become popular. Though these servers ran Linux, which isn't really DOS, started to spark an interest in DOS in a growing number of people. Gamers are actually a huge contributing cause to this, due to the fact that experience is required in the command line interface for players who want to host a server. Windows Server was, and as of today still is a popular server hosting operating system.

Decline in the use of DOS started in the mid-1990s, and from there it started to steadily decrease. Over the past few years, the usage, and community support of the command line has been at a steady low. With some spikes on the charts, the command line has found a way to live over 30 years of existence, which is quite impressive for a piece of software. Despite its decline, the command line is still a very useful tool to use, and a very powerful complement, and protection to have under your belt as well.

The continuation of the legacy of DOS will go on for quite some time. Basically, long as Windows exists, even it is no longer supported by Microsoft; themselves, the community base will keep it alive, and well. If fact, that's mainly how DOS has survived this 30 year dark period. DOS lived on through the support of the community surrounding it, and was supported by people who genuinely saw it for the art that is. The vast majority of people over the years have had little, to no interest in the command line, or DOS, but the continuous support from people who did take it seriously has kept it alive, all these years.

Unfortunately the vast majority of people fail to see what a great thing DOS was, and still is. This is the primary reason why DOS is starting to fade away into history. The GUI is great, but maybe it's viewed as a little *too* great. As its origin is becoming a thing of the past, and forgotten. After all, it is the command line, or DOS itself that enables the use of GUI. Do well to remember that all GUI is, is a graphical interface powered by commands, commands, and more commands.

Another reason why DOS has been fading could be its relevance, or lack of convenience. I'll admit using the command line isn't nearly as convenient as double-clicking an icon, or typing in a search bar to look for something. Sometimes, it's fairly unnecessary to even use the DOS, because of the ever fast moving development of technology, and troubleshooting methods. A lot of people aren't really convinced that the command line is an essential to computing, or an operating system, as it isn't really taught, advertised, or really even mentioned, all too much.

A lack of logical or rational reasoning of the public, really, has caused the downfall of DOS. Not to call anyone stupid, or anything, but mainly it's the refusal to acknowledge the deeper knowledge about computers science, networking, or really anything. It doesn't help at all that the average attention span is 8 seconds, and it doesn't take long to get bored with something as redundant, as the command line. It can be challenging at times. Leaning curves come, and people give up on it, a little too easy.

DOS – A True Art

It is important for a person to be computer savvy in terms of using the Command line interface and the Graphic user interface to interact with the machine. There are numerous advantages that are involved in learning how to use both interfaces. Each of them has their advantages and disadvantages.

Mastering both of them gives one an advantage in many scenarios. At work, with the use of numerous programs and operating in an intranet, the knowledge of the command prompt is quite important for the use to operate machines remotely and to ensure that high security standards are upheld. Additionally, the CLI offers a secure communication method between computers in a network, using the console.

DOS commands are a work of art whose master is the programmer or user of the computer. Although they may be viewed as difficult to execute and tedious to type the character-based input interface, it offers the author with the space to perform many more functions such as management of the files and manipulation of the computer functionalities. Additionally, there are important DOS commands that are still of great importance for users to learn. However, there are DOS systems still available for users, including, DR-DOS, FreeDOS and others. Additionally, the DOS structure encourages its use in embedded systems.

DOS does not have many programs that are compatible with

it. It is a platform for the programmers to create the programs they require as they work. The operating system is ideal for programmers. This is the basis for its consideration as an art. It allows programmers to exercise their different needs and create new programs and check their functionality while using them.

The programmer is able to improve on the work by identifying new functionalities. It is one method of learning how to create programs that do not need many graphical definitions. For cases where the program is unique to a specific function you need to execute, it is ideal as you can create a simple program for what you need.

For users who are not conversant with DOS command line, it is difficult to understand how the interface, which is at times regarded to as an out-dated method, is an art. There are many more functions that the command line can perform compared to the GUI interface.

DOS gives the real results rather than modifications and pretty illusions of executions that are given in the GUI interface. For instance, when a file is deleted using the GUI, it shows that space has been freed and gives the illusion that the file has been deleted from the hard drive.

However, it is common knowledge that the files are not deleted but taken to the inaccessible files directory. From here, they can be retrieved easily for use until the data is replaced appropriately.

However, in the case of the command line, the files are deleted and data is replaced immediately with other data so that the deleted information cannot be retrieved.

Additionally, for programmers, the command line is a platform for them to exercise their creativity as they seek for methods to execute functions that computer systems were not designed to perform initially. The command line can allow the programmer to chain command so that they are able to combine functions of different files, scripts and programs to execute something that would be too difficult or impossible to execute through the GUI interface.

Moreover, the command line also offers the ability to troubleshoot different components of the network and computer more extensively compared to the GUI interface. The programmer has the ability to adjust many options of the computer, including power, drivers and network devices and adaptors.

In networking, they enable troubleshooting of connections and to trace any malicious attacks that may be connected to the computer. This enhances security for the computer and the network in general. On the other hand, the GUI interface requires use of numerous programs to protect the computer and the entire network from malware and other attacks.

Furthermore, DOS systems have numerous applications that many who are aware of its applications would consider greatly important. For instance, DOS gaming is one of the main reasons why people consider using DOS emulators in Microsoft Windows. Additionally, the DOS system has several advantages for users even in the modern Microsoft systems.

There are many DOS based emulators available out there, many of which are easy to use, some of which more difficult. Either way, DOS is fairly open to new people, and has a welcoming community, for those who wish to learn how to use it.

The simplicity of DOS interface is its lightness and lack of need for excessive programs. DOS is small and can run on small space. This makes booting the system faster and easier. Additionally, DOS lacks the overhead of other operating systems that can multitask.

Although the main difference between the command line interface and the GUI is the time difference, DOS still has some advantages that it holds over the GUI. We shall highlight the advantages and disadvantages in order to help the users to determine which interface would be best for them. The disadvantages of DOS reflect the advantages of the GUI.

Advantages and disadvantages of DOS

Advantages

1. Use of the command line interface offers more control over different functions of the computer, including files and operating systems. For instance, a single line command can be used to transfer a file to a specific location. On the other hand, while GUI also offers simple transfer method, there are specific file transfers that need use of the command line interface. A programmer also has the ability to create new functionalities that would not be possible using singular commands.

2. The command line interface is the only method that guarantees ability to access a remote computer and manipulate the device content over a network.

3. The outlook and functionality of the command line is relatively more permanent compared to the GUI which changes its outlook with every update and new operating systems. This makes understanding DOS a more reliable interface once one masters how to use the command line. For instance, DOS commands that were used in the last century are still viable to date while GUI has had numerous changes in graphic appearance and icons.

4. For a user that is fast in typing, the command line interface is ideal as it does not involve use of the mouse which creates

distractions while multi-tasking between the keyboard and the mouse.

5. DOS offers more control over the computer components, including the hardware and software components. The command prompt allows one to manage the functionality of input devices, power components and other parts of the computer.

Disadvantages

1. It can be difficult to understand, especially for new users as it requires knowledge of the commands and how to use them. The GUI gains its main advantage from this due to its ease to understand and operate.

2. Multitasking is difficult compared to the ease of opening multiple windows, running software and manipulating multiple files open at the same time when using the GUI.

3. The command line makes system administrators prone to fatal errors due to loss of awareness of the information they work with. For instance, deleting the wrong file such as the system from the command line may cause great problems for them and the computing system.

Evidently, the use of the command line interface has numerous advantages compared to the GUI interface. The main reason why the GUI is preferred to the command line interface is the ease of understanding and multitasking. The ability for GUI to utilise different fonts, colours and graphics offers great abilities. However, the GUI is mostly effective for simple executions such as browsing and different media consumption. The GUI interface offers a clear situational awareness for system administrators and others users to identify and understand elements of information about the occurrences hence, avoiding errors.

The command line interface offers a powerful and programmable platform for the user to manipulate the device at more complex levels. Being programmable makes it most effective to perform repetitive tasks that would require a lot of repeated clicking and dragging using the mouse for the GUI.

The ability of the command line to handle complex tasks is the cause for its reference as an art. Despite the interface's fixed setting, the restrictions free the user from wasting time on things that are not important offering more time for the more complex and necessary functions. As artists put it, form liberates just as seen in this case.

Many command line interfaces also allow chaining of commands which extends the functions of the applications to beyond the functions that were designed for. This allows programmers to explore their creativity and create functions of scripts, commands and applications to perform tasks as they arise. In the GUI interface, this is not possible in most cases.

A piece of art allows the artist to express themselves in the best way possible. Art does not limit a person's functionality, only their imagination and creativity can limit them.

Similarly, when using DOS systems, the programmer is able to create new functionalities depending on their needs. The ability to use applications to perform functions that their designers did not have in mind is a creation of a new product in itself, which can be considered as a work of art.

While nobody can downplay the importance of GUI and the great impact it has had on user experience, it is important to learn DOS system. GUI interface is not a replacement for the command line interface; rather the two interfaces complement each other. In order to make more use of your computer, it is important to learn some important DOS commands that are vital in performing a variety of tasks. Here I'd like to run you through some of the most common and important DOS commands that every Microsoft user should memorise.

1. tasklist/taskkill

These are DOS commands that are used for troubleshooting the system. They are important for any user as the system is bound to have errors which will require troubleshooting that is dependent on deeper knowledge, rather than just using the simple programs that are offered by the GUI. One of the important commands is the "**tasklist**" command.

This command lists all active processes on your local or remote machine in real time. This can also be done in a more familiar fashion as this functionality is included in the GUI for windows known as the task manager; however is proven to be a more primitive way to manage your processes.

On the other hand, using the "**tasklist**" command enables you to use a variety of switches, and parameters that enable the user to manage their tasks, and processes in a more efficient manner. This can be done on either your personal machine, or on a remote machine via RDP (Remote Desktop Protocol). Furthermore the "**tasklist**" command has the ability to differentiate users on your systems, and manage their processes as well.

The "**taskkill**" command is fairly self-explanatory, as all it does is kill a specified task, as the name implies. Using the two of these commands together can not only teach you the ins and outs of managing tasks but can also be extremely useful, and powerful.

Command prompt displaying all currently running tasks

2. assoc.

This command is designed to point out files that are associated with a Specific Program. In windows, most files are associated with programs that open them.

For instance, typing the command "**assoc.doc**" will tell you the program the file extension is associated with. In this case Word, or how it would render: "**.doc=Word.Document.8**" for me. You also have the option to extend the command to specify the file associated with it.

For example, typing "**assoc.txt=Word.Document.8**" will change any file type ending with the extension ".txt" to automatically open in Microsoft Word, because now this file type is now associated with said program.

This is a simple and basic solution for situations in which you need to tell windows what program to run upon executing a file, or to change the associated file type to run on a different program.

This command is the GUI equivalent to the "Open with" menu. In other words, that menu you usually get when you double-click on a file that isn't known by your system. The menu looks like this:

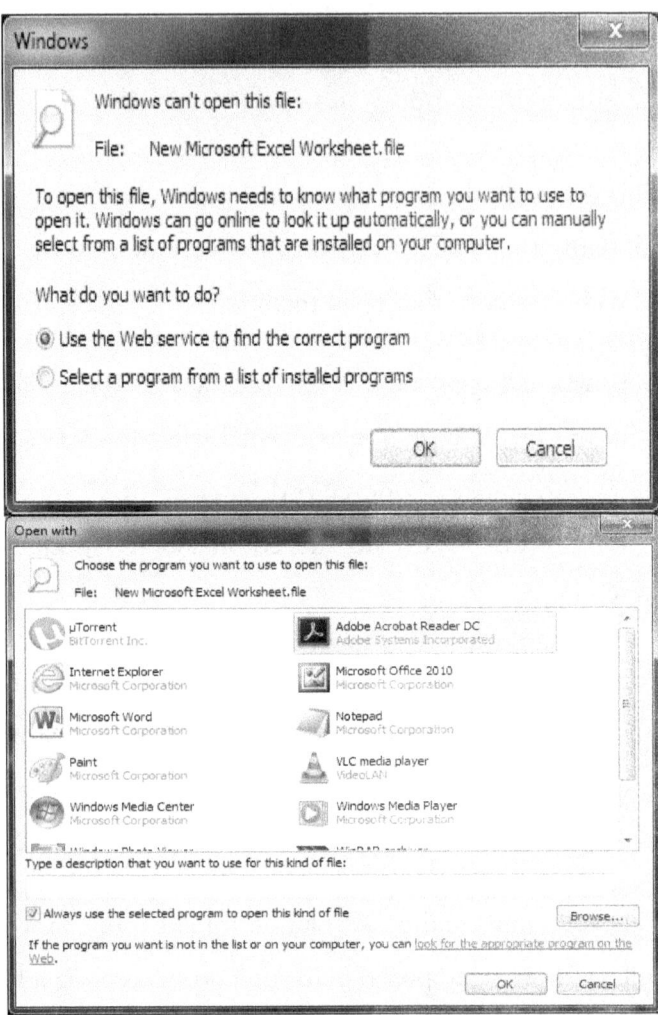

The GUI equivalent to the 'assoc' command

3. ipconfig(/all)

There are so many reasons why you need to know this command. I myself was surprised when I discovered how this command was so useful, and so powerful! The command has a number of functions that relate to your computers, and router's addresses.

For instance, the command in itself displays the computer's addresses. One might ask: "How many addresses are there?" or: "How many addresses do you need?" and those are both good questions. However, these are networking questions, which are a part of a whole different subject in itself.

With that said, let's keep this as simple as possible. A network needs to be organized so that each machine can send, and receive data, in the most efficient way. To do this, something called a *router* assigns different names (or addresses) to each machine on the network they are connected to.

The command "ipconfig" simply pulls information from your network interface, and displays your assigned information from said router. This information will include your machine's assigned IPv4 address, IPv6 address; routers address (also known as the default gateway). Typing the extension switch to this command "ipconfig/all" will display even more information such as the host name, MAC address (your physical machine's address), DHCP server address subnet mask, DNS server address, and more. Note: in case you use your computer over a router, it is the router's local network address that is displayed.

This command and others such as **netstat** are known as network commands. DOS tools used for troubleshooting networks are the most efficient. Also, specifying the "ipconfig/release" then "ipconfig/renew" will prompt the PC to request for a new IP address. This function is important for cases when the computer fails to identify its IP address.

Additionally, the "**ipconfig/flushdns**" command, also allows the user to refresh the DNS address. This command, also associated with the ipconfig, is most useful especially due to the tendency of Windows Network Troubleshooter to fail in its diagnosis.

Top:

Ipconfig showing information | Bottom: ipconfig/all showing more information

4. netstat

This is an external command that displays the TCP/IP network protocol information and statistics. It is also associated with the **"netstat-an"** command which displays the open ports at the time along with the associated IP address.

The command offers details of the state of the port in terms of whether it is closed, listening or established. It is an important command that helps you to troubleshoot network devices that are connected to the PC and also to locate a malicious connection that may have infected your computer with a Trojan.

I've run into many situations like this, I remember a couple times not knowing why I couldn't connect some of my games to public servers, or host my own servers on public server lists. It didn't take me long to figure out that the ports were not opened, and I had to forward them through my router, this is a common issue amongst games that are centred on multiplayer.

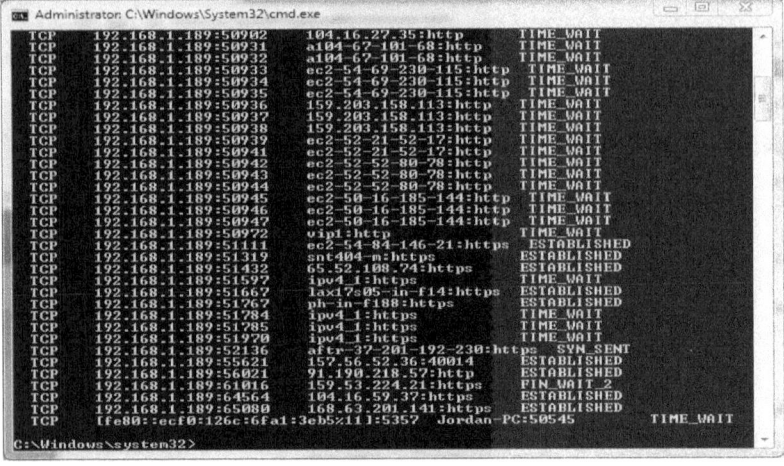

Top: netstat as shown in command prompt | Bottom: netstat -an as shown in command prompt

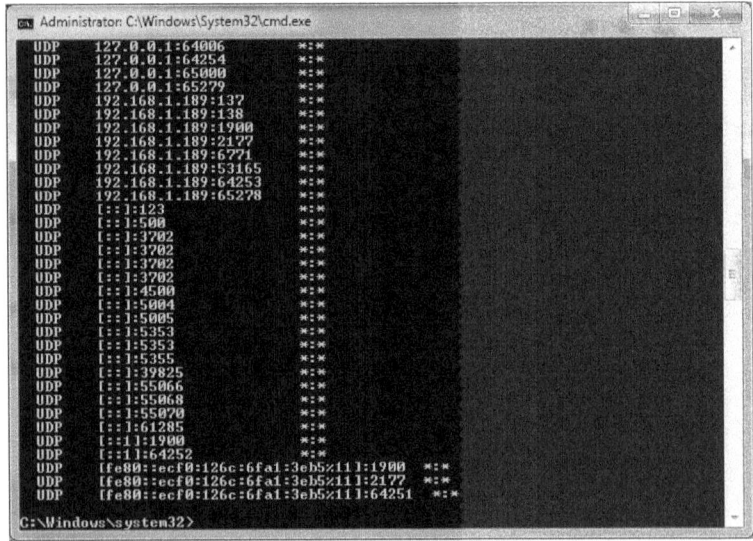

5. ping

This is probably the most commonly used command in the command line interface. It is useful in tracing packets that are being transferred whether or not they reach the specific device.

When using the command, you simply need to type PING followed by the IP address or domain whose connectivity you are trying to check. The ping command takes a packet to and from the device. If they fail, then you are able to identify cause of the failed connection.

Ever been in a situation where you didn't know if a printer, or router didn't have connectivity, or if it was your computer? The Ping command will let you know, though you might have to test it out on another computer.

```
Administrator: C:\Windows\System32\cmd.exe
Microsoft Windows [Version 6.1.7601]
Copyright (c) 2009 Microsoft Corporation. All rights reserved.

C:\Windows\system32>ping 192.168.1.1

Pinging 192.168.1.1 with 32 bytes of data:
Reply from 192.168.1.1: bytes=32 time<1ms TTL=64
Reply from 192.168.1.1: bytes=32 time<1ms TTL=64
Reply from 192.168.1.1: bytes=32 time<1ms TTL=64
Reply from 192.168.1.1: bytes=32 time<1ms TTL=64

Ping statistics for 192.168.1.1:
    Packets: Sent = 4, Received = 4, Lost = 0 (0% loss),
Approximate round trip times in milli-seconds:
    Minimum = 0ms, Maximum = 0ms, Average = 0ms

C:\Windows\system32>
```

Using "ping" to test connectivity of a router

6. cipher

This is the most effective method of clearing the computer memory. When files are deleted from the computer, they are not really deleted from the hard drive. The files are simply marked as inaccessible. The files are recoverable until they are overwritten with new data. Using the Cipher command wipes the data from a directory by writing data to it which takes a lot of time if the files are simply deleted.

The command is safe as it allows one to specify the directory path that should be erased. There are numerous cipher commands that are useable for similar reasons. They are, however unnecessary for Windows PC versions that have enabled Bitlocker. A simple example of using he cipher command to erase disk C, and that would be written as: "**cipher** /w:c".

```
Administrator: C:\Windows\System32\cmd.exe - cipher /w:C:\Program Files (x86)\screensavers\MS...
C:\Windows\system32>cipher /w:C:\Program Files (x86)\screensavers\MSD Galaxy Cla
ss Enterprise D
To remove as much data as possible, please close all other applications while
running CIPHER /W.
Writing 0x00
.......
```

Using "cipher" completely erases data of a specified directory

7. driverquery

This command is quite straightforward. As the name suggests, the command is used to query for errors within drivers in the PC. The command allows the user to view a list of all drivers installed in the device. This is an important command as it helps address the common problem in computers where we have drivers missing or wrongly configured.

The command also has several more commands associated with it that helps the user get more information on the drivers. For instance, the "**driverquery-v**" is used to view the drivers along with the directory it is located.

Using driverquery to display installed drivers

8. file compare

Commonly known as the fc command, it is used by programmers and other computer experts to trace the small differences between files, especially after software upgrades. The command has several extensions that allow one to specify the data they want to compare in the files, such as the binary output, the ASCII text and other details.

When executing the command, the command is simply

written in the format (fc /l "path directory of first file" "Path directory of second file"). The file extensions included are /b for binary output, /l for ASCII text. There are other extensions which are not covered in this example. I don't really have any notable experience with this command, but I find it to be extremely useful.

File comparison finding a slight difference in files

9. tree

This is the command that enables a person to locate the congruent of files and directories which is quite difficult to locate. The tree command allows you to view the directory structure. When you enter the directory whose structure you need, simply key in the command and file you want.

The complete directory structure is displayed in a format that can be printed out. This command is one of those commands that are used to look cool. I remember as a kid, I'd spam this command after typing in "**color 2**", to look like a hacker.

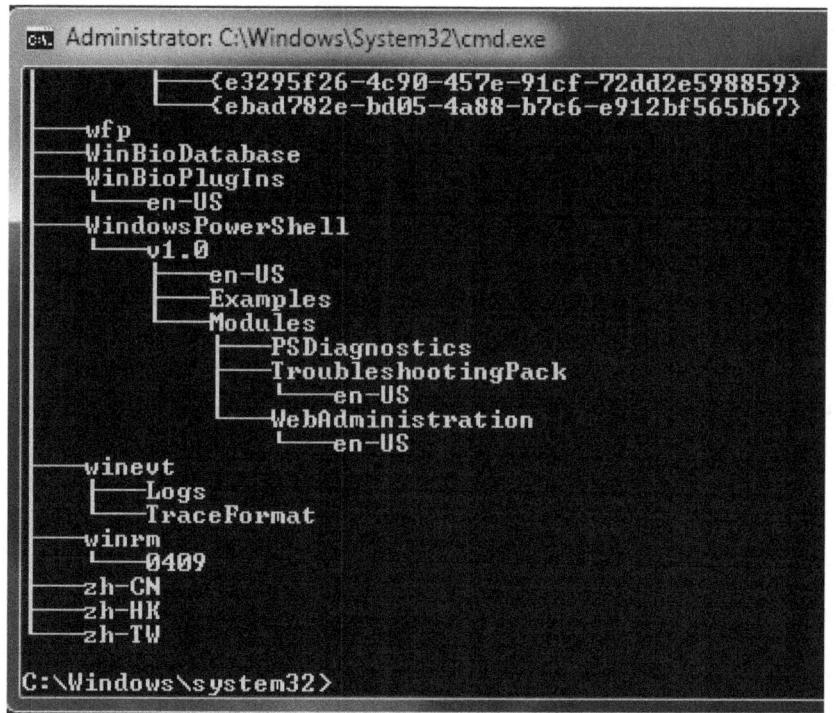

Tree, a graphical display of the directory structure

10. powercfg

This is an exceptional command that is used to track the computer's energy consumption and managing it. There are a variety of extensions that are related to the **powercfg** command. The user can manage the power saving states that are in the computer by using the "**powercfg /a**" command. One is also able to manage hibernation and also view the devices that support connections on standby and manage them so that they can start the computer remotely. The command for viewing these devices is the "**powercfg /devicequery s1_supported**".

Using this command, you can also follow up on the computer's usage by checking the time it was last used by using the "**Powercfg / lastwake**" command. There are numerous errors related to the computer's power consumption that can be tracked from this command and managed. For instance, a common power problem is computers' tendency to awake from sleep repeatedly by itself. The **powercfg /lastwake** command allows the users to check the frequency of the problem and helps the user learn how to manage it. The GUI offers its power management equivalent as the power options section in the control panel.

Powercfg

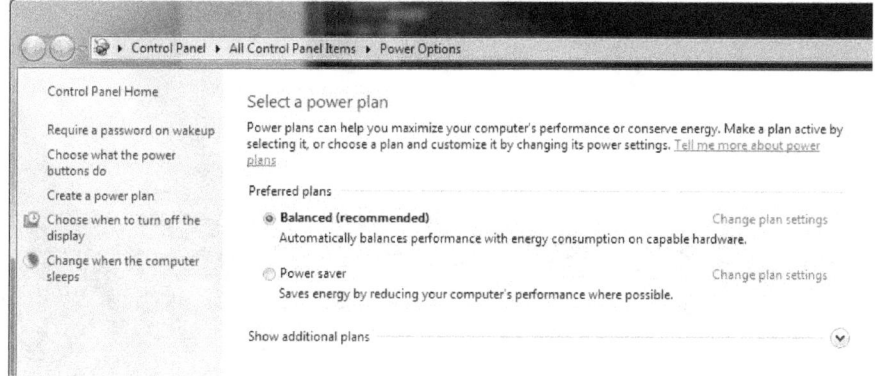

Power Management

11. at

This is a **classic example of ingenuity of the command prompt**. It is an external command that schedules a time to execute a particular program or program as set. It works as a reminder or sophisticated task scheduler. For instance, if I wanted to start the task manager at 6:50: PM I would type: "**at** 6:50PM "c:\windows\taskmanager.exe"".

There are some situations, where this would be helpful, especially if you are someone who is rather forgetful or busy during a day, and cannot remember when to do, something on windows. I know I was grateful to know about this command, when I had to fix a friend's computer from across the world that required a lot of restarts. You can also check all scheduled commands just by typing "at".

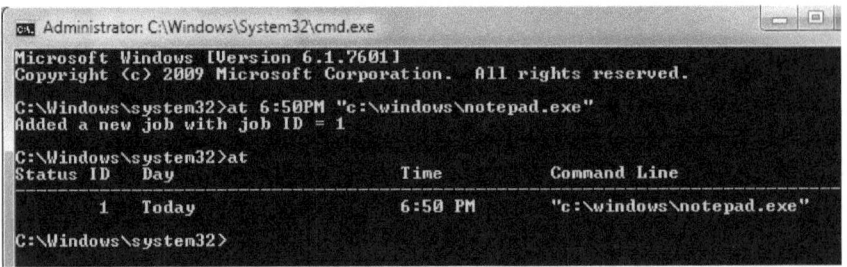

Using the at command to schedule a program to run

12. chkdsk (or chkntfs)

This is the command for checking for errors for hard drives running FAT. The **chkntfs** is the command that is used to check for errors in the NTFS hard drives.

These are functions that are rather difficult for the GUI user to execute as they need to understand the command prompt in order to understand even what the FAT and NTFS are. This command is extremely useful to be acquainted with, solely because it's a basic and simple way to check for major errors that make, or break an entire system.

```
Administrator: C:\Windows\System32\cmd.exe - chkdsk

C:\Windows\system32>chkdsk
The type of the file system is NTFS.
Volume label is Windows 7 Ultimate.

WARNING!  F parameter not specified.
Running CHKDSK in read-only mode.

CHKDSK is verifying files (stage 1 of 3)...
  238592 file records processed.
File verification completed.
  462 large file records processed.
  0 bad file records processed.
  2 EA records processed.
  64 reparse records processed.
CHKDSK is verifying indexes (stage 2 of 3)...
58 percent complete. (235899 of 297612 index entries processed)
```

Chkdsk

13. diskpart

This command executes a program within the command line that is used to manage disks, partitions, and volumes among windows. Within this program it's fluent, and easy to create, format, shrink, and extend, partitions, or volumes.

This command or program is very powerful in the effect that it is fully capable of wiping out tons of data, at a few keystrokes, so be careful. It's obvious that the GUI equivalent to this program is Disk Management. In my opinion **diskpart** is easier to use, than any GUI I've seen.

```
C:\Windows\system32\diskpart.exe

Microsoft DiskPart version 6.1.7601
Copyright (C) 1999-2008 Microsoft Corporation.
On computer: DANIEL-PC

DISKPART> list disk

  Disk ###  Status         Size     Free     Dyn  Gpt
  --------  -------------  -------  -------  ---  ---
  Disk 0    Online          931 GB     0 B
  Disk 1    Online          465 GB  1024 KB
  Disk 2    No Media          0 B      0 B
  Disk 3    No Media          0 B      0 B
  Disk 4    No Media          0 B      0 B
  Disk 5    No Media          0 B      0 B

DISKPART>
```

Managing disks, and partitions with diskpart

14. sfc/verifyfile

In cases where the computer recovers from a potential infection, the "**sfc** **/VERIFYFILE=**" command checks the authenticity of a file specified after the "=" sign. You can check for the authenticity of all files by using the '**sfc /scannow**' command. This is important, because system files have a tendency to fail, or get corrupted, especially after recovering from an infection, or virus.

15. tracert

Tracert, is an external command that is used to visually identify a network packet being sent, and received, also displaying the amount of hops required for said packet to reach its destination. **Tracert** is useful, because you can fully track its course to its destination.

For instance, if you had a network problem you could use the **tracert** command to see where your packets are stopping, and this would help you isolate the problem. The **tracert** command is often used with other networking related Command Prompt commands like **ping**, **ipconfig**, **netstat**, **nslookup**, which are also, very useful commands.

```
Administrator: C:\Windows\System32\cmd.exe

Microsoft Windows [Version 6.1.7601]
Copyright (c) 2009 Microsoft Corporation.  All rights reserved.

C:\Windows\system32>tracert google.com

Tracing route to google.com [216.58.216.14]
over a maximum of 30 hops:

  1    <1 ms    <1 ms    <1 ms  router.asus.com [192.168.1.1]
  2     *        *        *     Request timed out.
  3    14 ms    17 ms    13 ms  100.127.2.72
  4    10 ms    10 ms    11 ms  24-234-6-28.ptp.lvcm.net [24.234.6.28]
  5    25 ms    23 ms    24 ms  sanjbprj02-ae0.0.rd.sj.cox.net [68.1.5.186]
  6    30 ms    25 ms    27 ms  ip70-167-151-23.at.at.cox.net [70.167.151.23]
  7    36 ms    33 ms    48 ms  108.170.242.82
  8    36 ms    25 ms    23 ms  209.85.246.20
  9    29 ms    25 ms    27 ms  64.233.174.204
 10    49 ms    32 ms    29 ms  64.233.175.151
 11    22 ms    23 ms    27 ms  216.239.50.233
 12    23 ms    35 ms    34 ms  108.170.237.185
 13    31 ms    30 ms    30 ms  lax02s21-in-f14.1e100.net [216.58.216.14]

Trace complete.

C:\Windows\system32>
```

Tracing packets to google.com

CONCLUSION

In the end however, DOS really is just another operation system, and another piece of software, telling other pieces of hardware what to do, and how to do it, though it is sad to say. Truly, DOS' entrance into the world was a miracle, in itself. In reality, we're able to communicate with computes, over thin layers of copper that are literally inches in width, and depth, over mere electrical signals. Really, this is a cutting edge technology, and still is amazing as it was back in the day.

DOS came into the world in 1981, of August, and still lives on today. It's had a nice long and healthy lifespan, and even now has a hopeful legacy, Windows, and the command line. If I had to predict what was going to happen, I'd say that DOS isn't going anywhere, anytime soon, based just off of gamers, and their will to learn how to expand their growing knowledge of computers, and technical based skillsets.

With the release of DOS, the world started to change in terms of technology, for the better. New, and ground-breaking technologies, started to emerge from their shadows, as well as new, and improved software developments, and developers stated to rise to the occasion. The world certainly changed, when DOS came to light.

Though GUI was, and still is a wonderful feature of an operating system, nothing will ever undermine, nor trump the originality, of DOS, which makes all else possible. DOS shall never go forgotten as the building block and infrastructure to any GUI within windows, and should definitely be recognized for what it was, and is, a piece of art.

DOS will continue for some time, as I said before. The communities surrounding it, the people who appreciate it, and people who are learning it, and especially the people who are using it, and modifying it are definitely all doing their part to keep it alive and well, and I sure hope I have helped this cause, as I fully appreciate, and admire what DOS was, is, and what it has yet to be.

DOS is a mark, and a reminder that we all live in very exciting times, in terms of technology. It also serves, as one of the Founding Fathers to what we know today as operating systems, and software itself. Let us never forget the start that Microsoft gave us with DOS; let us come together, and restore…

The Lost Art of DOS Commands!

ABOUT THE AUTHOR

Daniel Valencia, is an upcoming IT specialist who began his career at age 14, when his father introduced him to the business world. Daniel now resides in Henderson, Nevada, where he works as an IT Tech.

Jordan Kaufman has almost two decades of experience in technology centered primarily around enterprise software, audio engineering, and alternative animation techniques.

Kaufman also recently started an online community called www.SixFigureTeen.com which promotes youth entrepreneurship, education and alternatives to college.

He resides in the American Southwest with his amazingly supportive wife and family.

jordanrkaufman@gmail.com
Twitter: @Jordan_RK

www.ingramcontent.com/pod-product-compliance
Lightning Source LLC
Chambersburg PA
CBHW061448180526
45170CB00004B/1610